SCHIRMER'S LIBRARY OF MUSICAL CLASSICS

OTAKAR ŠEVČIK

Op. 1

School of Violin Technics

Edited by

PHILIPP MITTELL

IN FOUR PARTS

→ Part I: Exercises in the First Position
Library Vol. 844

Part II: Exercises in the Second to Seventh Positions
Library Vol. 845

Part III: Shifting (Changing the Position)
Library Vol. 846

Part IV: Exercises in Double-Stops
Library Vol. 847

G. SCHIRMER, *Inc.*

Erster Teil.

Erste Lage.

Fingerübungen auf einer Saite.

Man wiederhole jeden Takt mehrere Male, langsam und schnell, gestossen und gebunden, und achte, dass die Finger gleichmässig und fest aufschlagen. Siehe Anmerkung zu Op. 8.

Part First.

First Position.

Finger-exercises on One String.

Repeat each measure several times, both slowly and quickly, *détaché* and legato; and be careful that the fingers make the stops evenly and firmly. Read the Remarks at the head of Opus 8.

1.

*) Die Finger fest liegen zu lassen.

*) Keep the fingers down firmly.

2.

3.

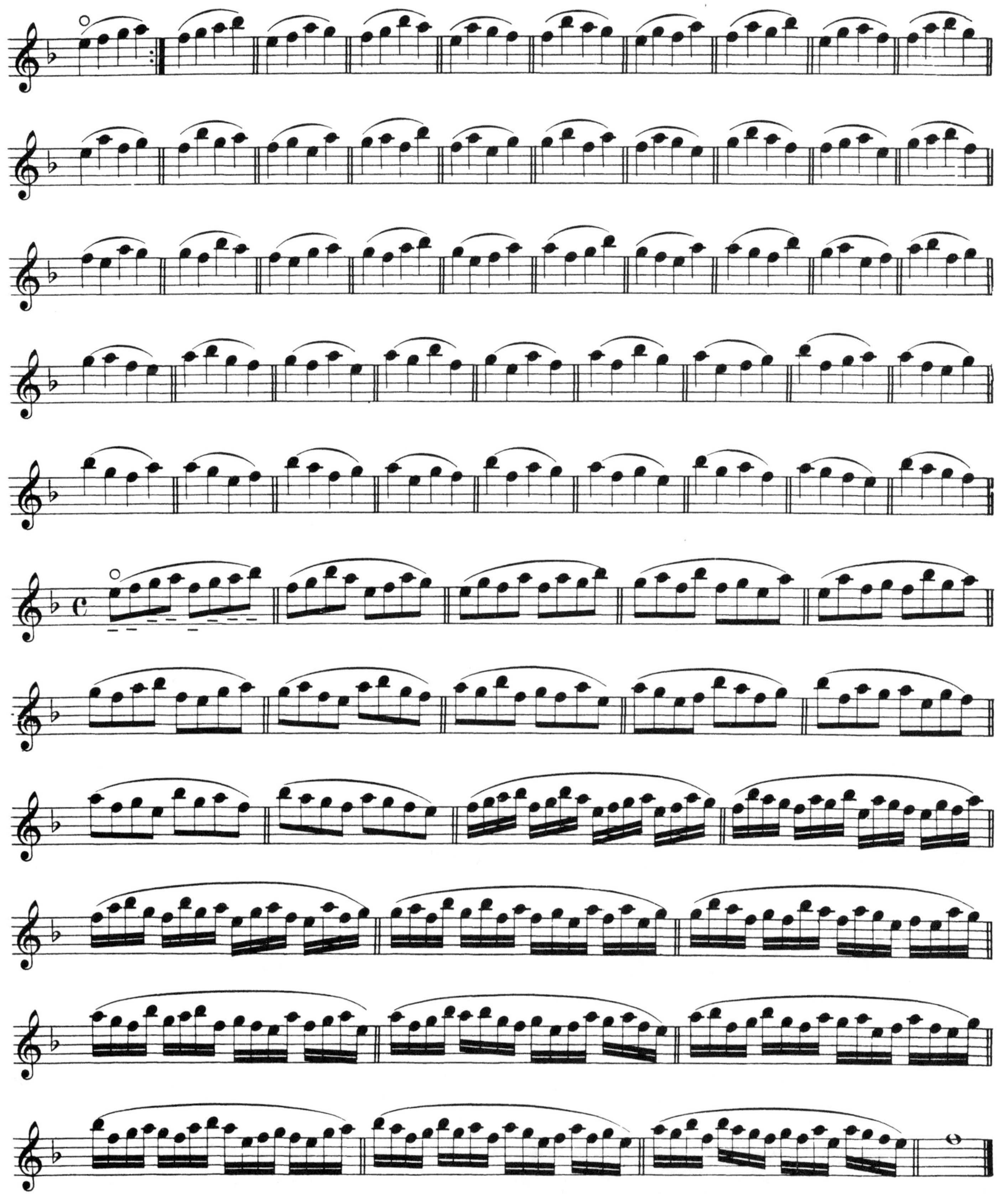

4.

Man wiederhole zuerst jeden Takt einzeln, dann zu zweien.

Repeat each measure by itself at first; then 2 together.

5.

6.

7.

*) Diese Übungen sollen auf jeder Saite geübt werden. | *) Practise these exercises on each string.

9.

10.

Übungen auf zwei Saiten.	Exercises on Two Strings.
Man wiederhole zuerst jeden Takt einzeln, dann zu zweien.	Repeat each measure by itself at first; then 2 together.

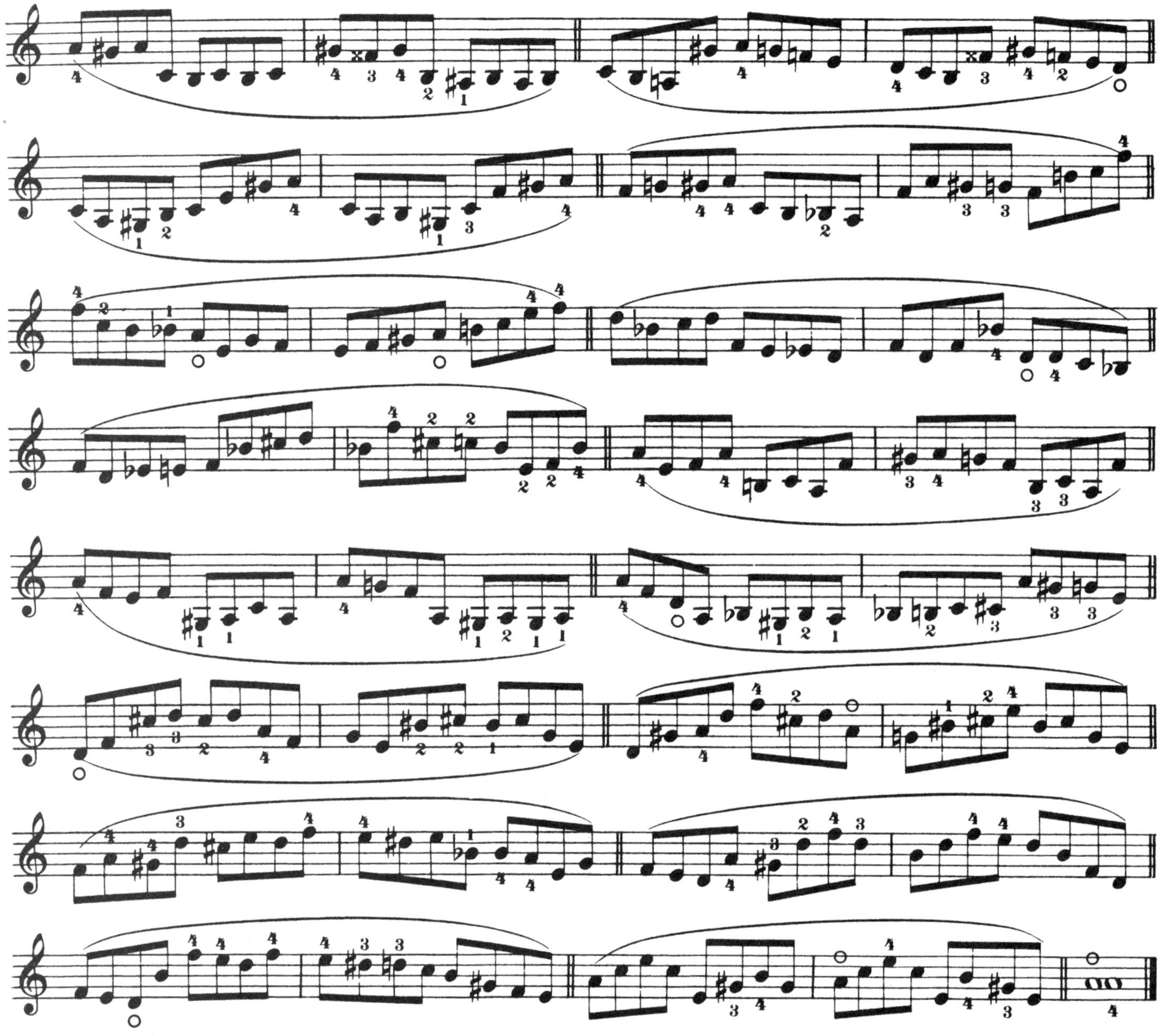

11.*)

Übung des rechten Handgelenks.

Dieses Beispiel ist mit allen folgenden Stricharten auszuführen.

Practice for the Right Wrist.

Practise this exercise with each of the bowings marked below.

Beispiel:
Example:

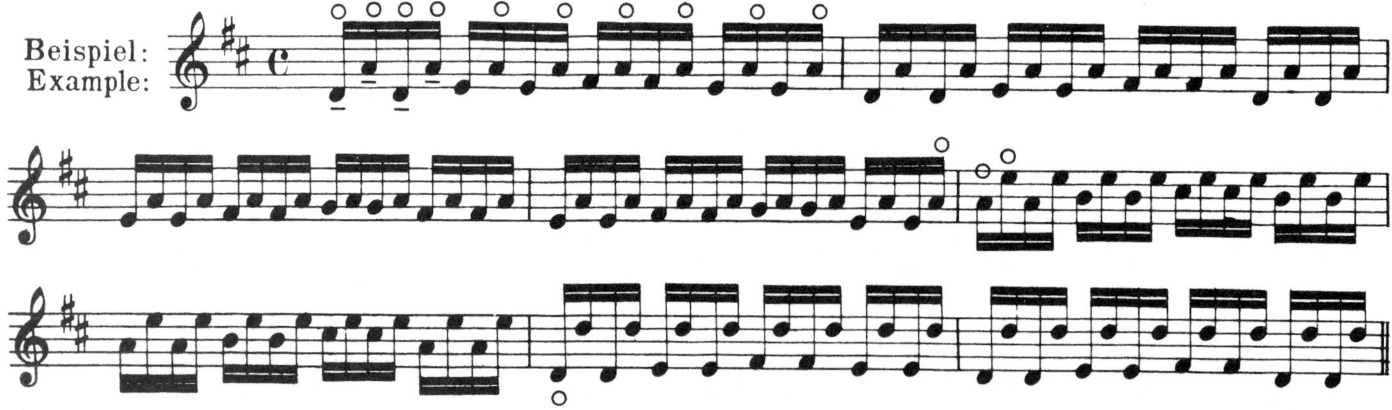

*) Man übe diese Übung langsam in der Mitte, dann erst an der Spitze und am Frosch.

*) Practise this exercise slowly in the middle of the bow; after this, at the point and the nut.

*) Auch sind die harmonischen Tonleitern zu üben. | *) Also practise the harmonic scales.

13.

Tonleitern in Terzen.

Die eingeklammerten Zeichen ♯, ×, ♮, sind nur bei der Wiederholung der einzelnen Moll-Tonleitern zu beachten.

Scales in Thirds.

The signs (♯),(×) and (♮) are to be observed only at the repetition of the minor scales.

14.
Übung in Sexten.
Exercise in Sixths.

15.

Oktaven. | Octaves.

16.

Nonen, Dezimen u.a. | Ninths, Tenths, etc.

Die Finger sind möglichst lange liegen zu lassen. | Keep the fingers down as long as possible.

17.

Dreiklang. | Tonic Triads.

18.*) **)

Diese Übung ist mit jeder Strichart ganz auszuführen.

Sp. An der Spitze } des Bogens.
Fr. Am Frosch } des Bogens.
G.B. Mit ganzem Bogen.

This entire exercise is to be practised with each of the given bowings.

Pt. Near the Point } of the bow.
Nut Near the Nut } of the bow.
W.B. Whole bow.

*) Die Finger liegen lassen.
**) Diese Uebung soll zuerst gestossen geübt werden.

*) Keep the fingers down.

19.

Chromatische Tonleiter. | Chromatic Scale.

20.

Verminderter Septimenakkord.

Die ganzen Noten sind zu greifen, ohne gespielt zu werden.

Chord of the Diminished Seventh.

Hold down the whole notes without playing them.

21.

22.

Verschiedene Akkorde arpeggirt. | Arpeggios of Different Chords.

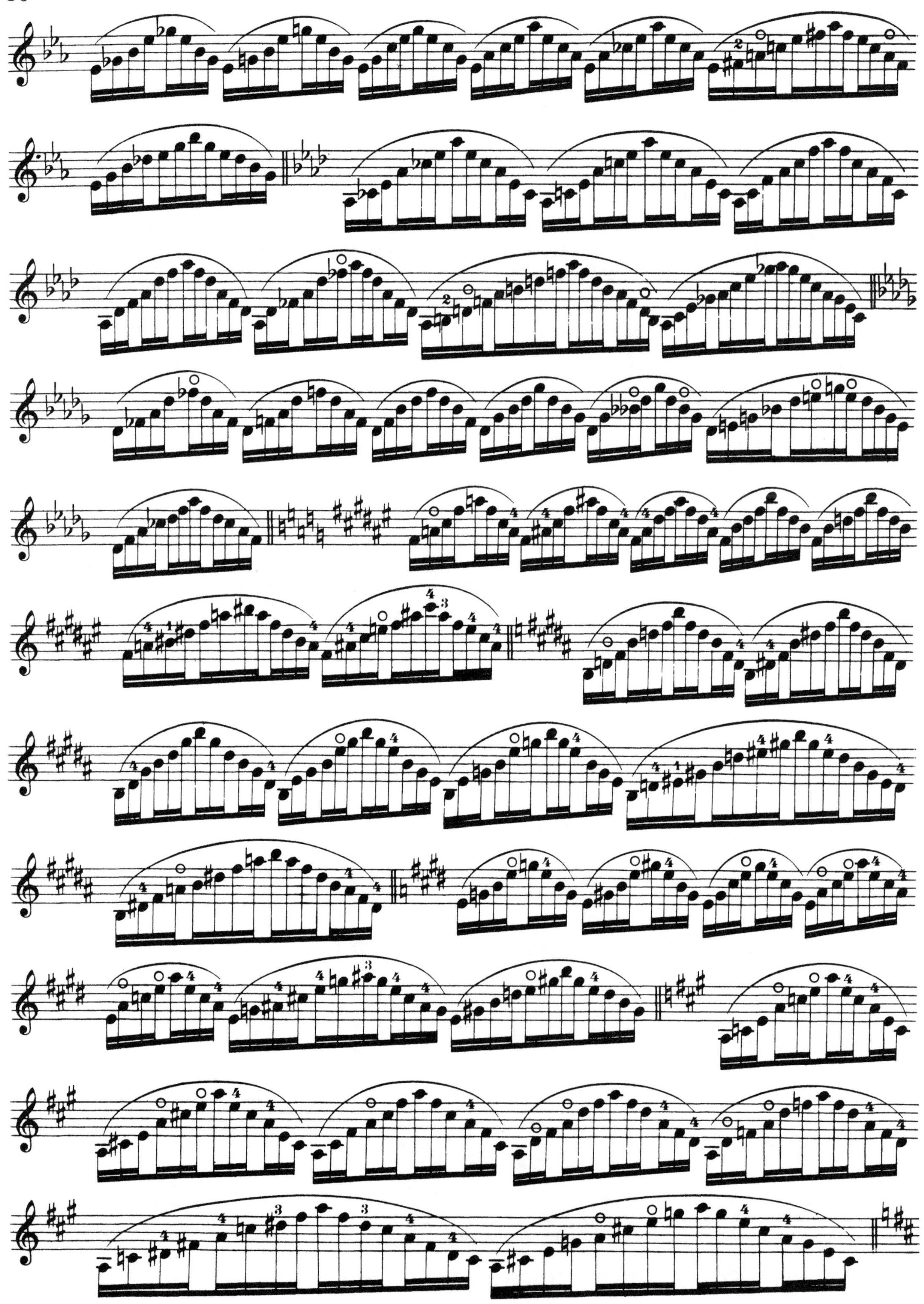

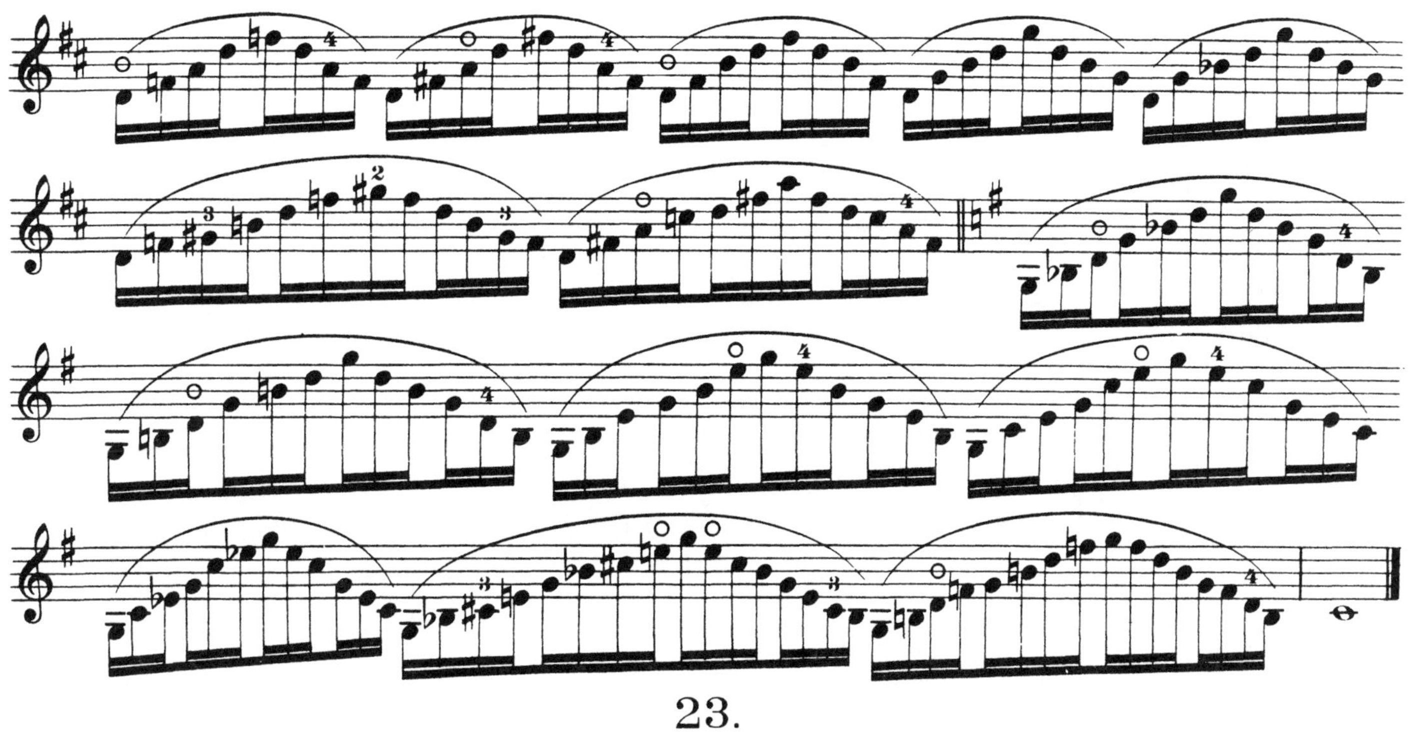

23.

Übungen in Doppelgriffen. | Exercises in Double-stops.

24.

25.

26.
Beispiele in allen Tonarten.
Exercises in All Keys.

27.

Übung in Akkorden. Exercises in Chords.

27.

Dieselbe Übung mit schwierigeren Akkorden. | The Same, with more difficult chords.

29.

Übung in verschiedenen Stricharten.

Erklärung der Zeichen:

Sp.	An der Spitze	des Bogens.
M.	In der Mitte	
Fr.	Am Frosch	
Fr. z...... Sp.	Vom Frosch bis zur Spitze	
Fr. z...... M.	Vom Frosch bis zur Mitte	
M. z...... Sp.	Von der Mitte bis zur Spitze	
H. B.	Mit halbem Bogen.	
G. B.	Mit ganzem Bogen.	

Exercise in Various Bowings.

Explanation of the Signs.

Pt.	Near the Point	of the bow.
M.	Near the Middle	
Nut	Near the Nut	
N. to..... Pt.	From Nut to Point	
N. to..... M.	From Nut to Middle	
M. to..... Pt.	From Middle to Point	
H. B.	With half the bow.	
W. B.	With whole bow.	

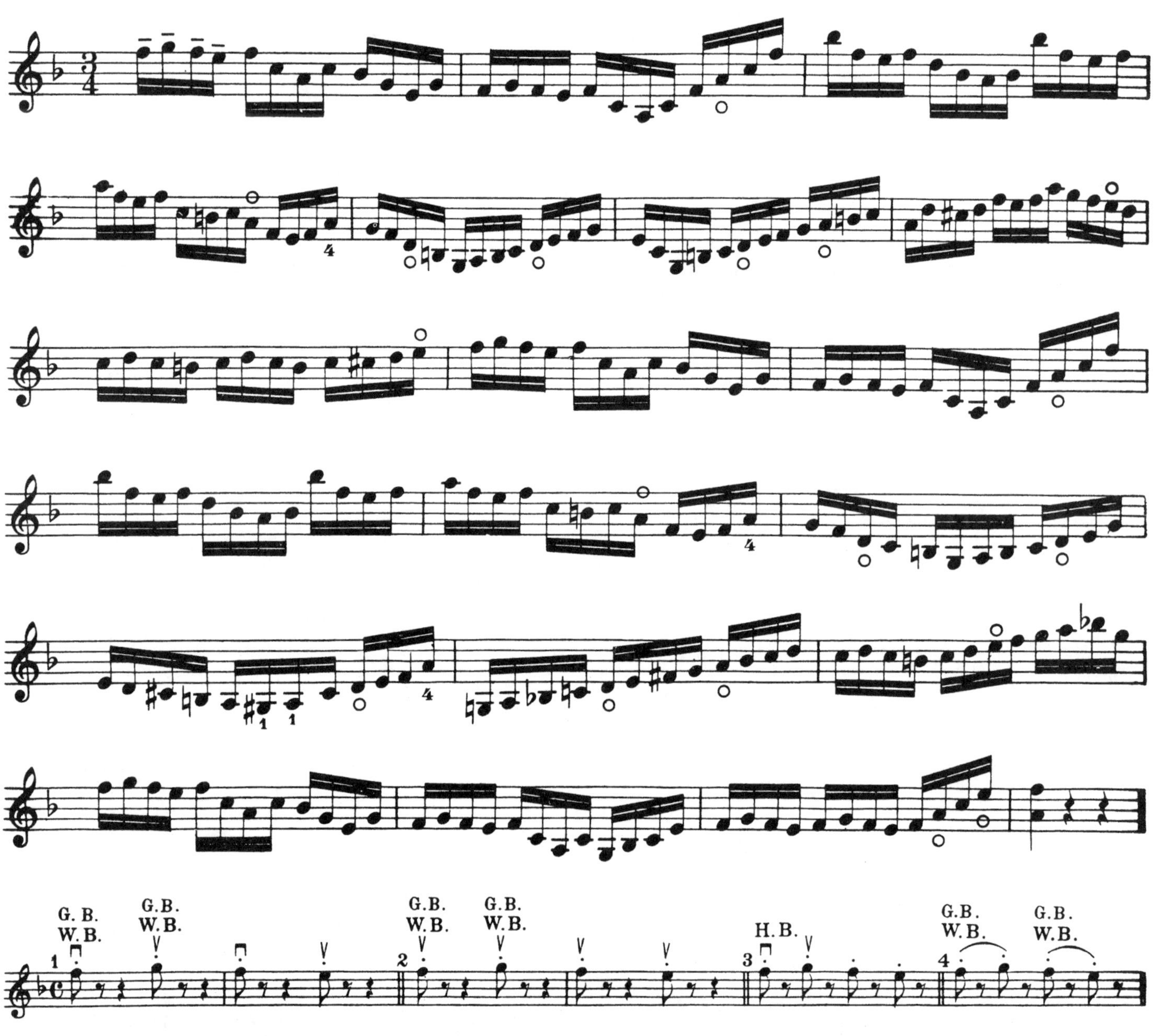

5 G. B. W. B. — 6 Sp. Pt. *martelé* — 7 Fr. Nut *martelé* — 8 M. *spiccato*

9 Fr. Nut G. B. W. B. Sp. Pt. G. B. W. B. — 10 Fr. Nut G. B. W. B. Sp. Pt. G. B. W. B. — 11 Fr. Nut — 12 Fr. Nut

13 Fr. Nut — 14 Fr. Nut — 15 Fr. Nut — 16 Fr. Nut — 17 Fr. Nut — 18 Fr. Nut — 19 Fr. Nut

20 Fr. Nut — 21 Fr. Nut — 22 Fr. Nut — 23 Fr. Nut — 24 Fr. Nut

25 Fr. Nut — 26 Fr. Nut — 27 Fr. Nut G. B. W. B. G. B. W. B. — 28 Sp. Pt. G. B. W. B. G. B. W. B.

29 M. zu Sp. M. to Pt. H. B. — 30 Fr. Nut H. B. H. B. — 31 Sp. Pt. — 32 Fr. Nut — 33 M. H. B. H. B. — 34 H. B. H. B. — 35 Sp. Pt. H. B. H. B. — 36 M. H. B.

37 Sp. Pt. H. B. H. B. — 38 M. H. B. H. B. H. B. — 39 Sp. Pt. — 40 Fr. Pt. — 41 G. B. W. B. G. B. W. B. — 42 Sp. Pt. — 43 Sp. Pt. — 44 Fr. z. M. N. to M. H. B.

45 Fr. to M. N. to M. H. B. — 46 Sp. Pt. H. B. H. B. — 47 H. B. — 48 Sp. Pt. G. B. W. B. — 49 H. B. — 50 Fr. Nut — 51 Sp. G. B. Pt. W. B. — 52 Sp. Pt.

53 M. H. B. — 54 M. H. B. — 55 Fr. z. M. N. to M. H. B. — 56 Fr. Nut G. B. W. B. — 57 M. H. B. H. B. — 58 Fr. z. M. N. to M. H. B. — 59 Fr. z. M. N. to M. H. B. — 60 G. B.

61 M. z. Sp. M. to Pt. H. B. — 62 M. z. Fr. M. to N. H. B. — 63 Sp. Pt. — 64 Fr. Nut — 65 Fr. z. N. to .... Sp. Pt. — 66 Fr. Nut M. H. B.

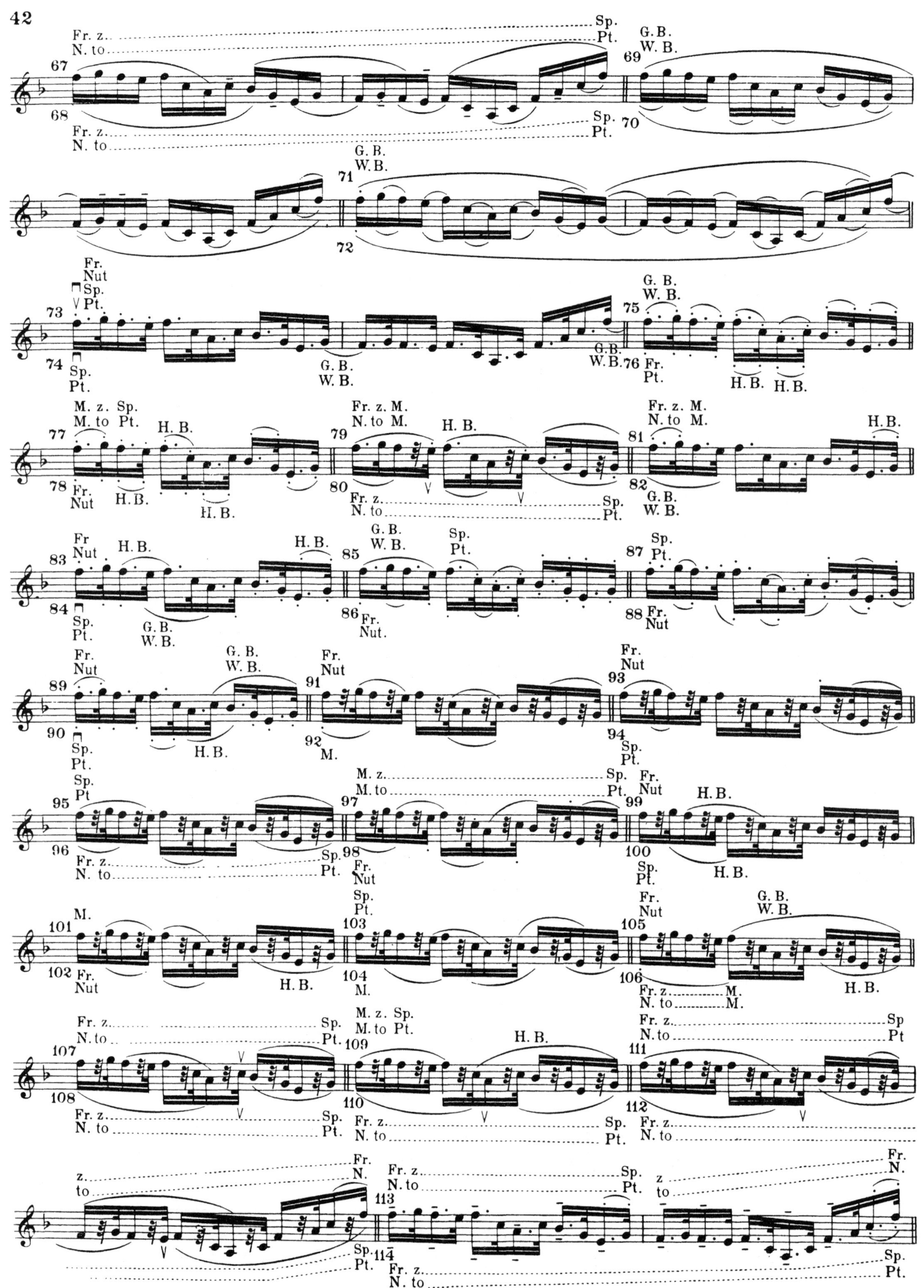

M.
Fr.
Nut
115
116
117
118
119
120
121
122
123
124
125
126
127
128
129
130
131
132
133
134
135
136
137
138
139
140
141
142
143
144
145
146
147
148
149
150
151
152
M.
153
spiccato
M.
spiccato
154
155
156
157
M.
158
159
M.
160
161
M.
sautillé
162
163
M.
164
sautillé
165
ricochet
166
167
168
169
170